To June!!

A new angel in
my life!
We will meet
again —

Jhone

Your Psychic Says...

Johanne Verville-Huffaker

authorHOUSE®

AuthorHouse™
1663 Liberty Drive, Suite 200
Bloomington, IN 47403
www.authorhouse.com
Phone: 1-800-839-8640

First published by AuthorHouse 9/4/2007

ISBN: 978-1-4343-3047-5 (sc)

Library of Congress Control Number: 2007906029

Printed in the United States of America
Bloomington, Indiana

This book is printed on acid-free paper.

Your Psychic Says...

The Book that gives you instant insight

Over my years as a practicing psychic, thousands have come to me for readings. I have become acutely aware of the limits of time to respond to so many questions and needs. More and more I thought, "How can I help everyone by giving them a source of instant insight"?

So, I created this book where every page contains a message. This may be for a question or concern you have, but also can apply to something coming into your life. The book is created by pure intuition so that when joined with your own energy, you can be led to what you need to hear at the moment. Some of you will find it accurate and helpful, and others will find it entertaining. I know from my own experience, it all depends on intent and ones spiritual connection.

Even so, this book is not intended to take the place of a full reading session. As those who have had a session with me know, in-depth treatment of issues and concerns lay the foundation for major decision making on the part of a client. So it goes almost without saying, that if your concerns go beyond the scope of this book, I recommend a session with me. This can be by a personal appointment, either in my office, or by phone from anywhere in the world.

These messages can give you hope and insight. It will also open your thinking to your potential, making it fascinating and fulfilling!

Writing this book has been pure pleasure for me. I
hope all of you reading this book will love using it as
much I have in creating it!

Johanne Verville-Huffaker

www.joverville.com

Disclaimer:

The author of this book does not dispense medical advice or prescribe the use of any technique as a form of treatment for emotional or physical medical problems. The intent of the author is only to offer information of a non-medical nature to help you in your quest for emotional and spiritual well-being. Neither the author nor the publisher can assure your desired results from the use of this book. In the event that you use the information in this book for yourself, which is your constitutional right, the author and the publisher assume no responsibility for your actions.

Acknowledgements

I would like to thank my darling husband, Dale, for his untiring encouragement in whatever I choose to do, including writing this book.

The experiences of reading so many clients in the past two decades have provided a fountain of insight for me to draw on as I wrote this book. I would have an incredible list of people's names if I were to thank everyone who has given me the privilege of working with them.

I would also like to recognize the amazing encouragement and support from my friends, Vicki Hiley (who took the photo for the front cover), Jill Heerensperger, Sandy Brewer, Joanne Demers, Betty Batista, J. Russell, Sandi Williams, Jean Batson, Carol Young, Susan Kerr, Angie Ring, Deanne McFann, Patty Service, Fredrick Child, Michele Karen, Frank Torok and Dan McGrath. Always in specifically naming names, I am sure some will have escaped me at the moment. Please unmentioned friends, do not be hurt. Being a psychic does not provide a perfect memory in my personal life, and I must get this to the publisher.

My family has also been very supportive and excited watching the progress of this book. They include my sisters, Michele Audet, Celine Dallaire and dearest brother, Alain Verville; as well as my sisters in law, Bonnie Huffaker and Kitt Huffaker.

I love many people who have made their transition to the next life, and I know some are deeply involved with my work. I acknowledge especially my father, Bruno Verville, who was a great inspiration and so very proud of me; and my amazing mother, Lise Verville, who was the best psychic I ever met. They were looking over my shoulder while every word of this book was written.

Thanks, Mom and Dad!

How to Use This Book

Sit quietly and think about your need. You must be clear about what you desire, or the concern you have.

Holding this book with both hands, quietly ask your question or state your concern. With eyes closed, fan the book pages back and forth with your thumbs or fingers feeling the edge of the pages, and then randomly open the book to where you are inclined. Remember, it is your spiritual energy that directs you to the page intended for you.

If the response does not seem logical for now, it may well apply to future events that have not yet occurred. If you missed entirely, you can go through the same process again, voicing the same question or concern, but worded differently this time. Or maybe you are trying too hard, and a better connection to your intuitive self comes in releasing your stress along with relaxing your mind.

Once connected, your intuition will most assuredly direct you to a page meant for you.

If there is no special question, you may want to use this book just to see what message is given for that day.

Enjoy!

Draw on your own foresight and resourcefulness to make decisions that will further your ambitions in life. A path of great fulfillment is ahead. Let your major headline be that you initiate positive change in many areas of your life.

Your Psychic Says .....

There is so much more to be gained by letting go of yesterday's challenges. You have learned from them, but are not stymied. New ideas are always as near as your next thought. I see you now progressing with your creative thinking.

Your Psychic Says .....

I see you overextending yourself. You need to have some quiet times. When you are rested and at peace, you radiate the kind of energy that is you. Your stress energy does not help you any. Time for you to get more solid with the real you.

Your Psychic Says .....

More and more, you'll have the opportunity to see where a new path takes you. Remember that progress would be impossible if you always did things the way you always have. Deep within you, feel a promise of fulfillment. Hang on to that feeling.

Your Psychic Says .....

Refuse to allow yourself to have low expectations. Let this be a time to enter a more passionate and creative phase in your life. Start creating the conditions you desire. Be strong, independent, positive, and you can put these feelings to good use. Bask in the love and admiration of friends and family around you.

Your Psychic Says .....

Though all the things in your environment are not in your control, do the best you can with what you've got.

Your Psychic Says .....

Someone is looking out for you. Things are not always what they seem. Some situations call for more of the mental than the physical game.

Your Psychic Says .....

Put your ideas into motion knowing that your creative energy is at its strongest. Take full advantage of this great phase. The future is something to look forward to. Fill yourself with a sense of positive expectation concerning the success lying ahead.

Your Psychic Says .....

As you resolve your anxieties, you are set to focus on the journey ahead. You are ready to broaden your horizon. Someone new comes into your life and helps you reflect on this expansive time. Why not get a few travel brochures and plan a trip?

Your Psychic Says .....

A new beginning is here. It is time for decision-making and action. You must use your intuitive insight to make the right decision. Be willing to trust that whatever you choose will be worthwhile and meaningful.

Your Psychic Says .....

Life often seems slow with very little excitement, but I see this as a time for you to enjoy the simple pleasures. Travel, reunion and fun times are here. Do not be in such a rush. Enjoy!

Your Psychic Says .....

Acknowledge the existence of a higher power and allow yourself to rely on it for support. Listen to that inner voice that guides you. I see you receiving dreams that will inspire you in your life.

Your Psychic Says .....

Everything is going according to the plan. Stay focused on what you want and where you want to go. I see that you will be reaping the rewards of your endeavors. Feel good about who you are now.

Your Psychic Says .....

You may feel embattled, but I see you having the strength to overcome the situation. You have the skill and resilience to deal with the opposition you are facing. Dig into your energy reserves.

Your Psychic Says .....

Be honest with yourself and come to terms with what has gone wrong. You have a chance to learn more about yourself. What you are going through is a prerequisite to your growth, laying the foundation for happier times.

Your Psychic Says .....

Hang it up - or hang in there! Only you can decide whether it is better to stay where you are. Sleep on it for now.

Your Psychic Says .....

I see you studying or taking up a new interest that inspires you. There are lots of books and papers around you. It will be quite time consuming, and you will welcome some help. For quality assistance of this kind, search places you have heretofore not been very familiar with.

Your Psychic Says .....

Money falls out of your pocket. Quit pouring it down the drain. It is time to get back on your feet. Changes in spending or saving patterns are required, NOW! All the ingredients are there to turn your financial situation to your advantage. But you must make the choice.

Your Psychic Says .....

Companionship! It is time you sought out yours. Someone looks at you with starry eyes. Or perhaps you need to make this an opportunity for renewing the commitment you made to your soul mate. As a result, I see your love life fresh and new again.

Your Psychic Says .....

You have a lot to be grateful for. Embrace the moment! This is a rewarding time that brings with it a feeling of great happiness. Count your blessings. Give thanks. Why not call someone right now and tell them how grateful you are to have them in your life?

Your Psychic Says .....

Whether or not you are actually rich, this is a good day to dress and accessorize as if you are. I see that as you adopt this image, the wealth vibrations increase. I predict a raise or monetary gift coming to you just when you need it.

Your Psychic Says .....

I see you on the threshold of taking a fresh direction. I sense that you are starting a new career or business, and are eager to get going. However, do not be in too much of a rush, for impulsive decisions will undermine your success.

Your Psychic Says .....

I see that reconciliation is possible if you are willing to forgive and forget. Put the friendship or relationship on a fresh footing. It is a time for healing and creating a strong bond.

Your Psychic Says .....

Don't believe everything you hear! Someone really doesn't have your best interests at heart. Read between the lines. There is no truth to some of the rumors on the grapevine. Be suspicious of someone with dark eyes.

Your Psychic Says .....

I sense that you have a tendency for leaping first and thinking later, or to buy now and pay later. This is leaving you scattered and spread too thin. Take Charge!

Your Psychic Says .....

You are looking forward to something you have planned for the weekend. Do something nice for yourself - you deserve it. There is more than a possibility you will "get lucky" with love. It marks the beginning of a relationship or a new stage in an existing one.

Your Psychic Says .....

I see your door of opportunity opening up. Don't let it close in your face again. Offers like this don't come along every day. Go for it.

Your Psychic Says .....

You can never tell when a personal contact will prove useful. I see you being invited for lunch or dinner where small talk will go a long way. That is the way good things start.

Your Psychic Says .....

I sense that you are learning new ways through the inevitable ups and downs of life. Someone is in a position to help you, and will do so. Good things are lining up for you.

Your Psychic Says .....

Getting away right now is well worth it. In fact, it may be some of the best money you ever spent. You will return from the trip with a fresh perspective on life. You need it!

Your Psychic Says .....

I sense that you will meet someone important while traveling or relocating. This person is coming into your life to bring opportunities that can take you to new places. A seed will be planted for change.

Your Psychic Says .....

I see difficult issues that can now be resolved, if you are willing to honor your own domain, boundaries, and limits you have created for yourself. But it is important to look afresh at what your limits and boundaries are. Write them down, and look at them often. The issues will be clearer. So will your decisions.

Your Psychic Says .....

It is time to get clear on your priorities. Determine what it is you want. Once you are clear on that, stick with it. This then becomes your vision of life, followed by a reality that matches it.

Your Psychic Says .....

I see that the time has come to have a day alone. Ignore other's demands. It is all about "You". This is a day when you might consider healing and restoring your energy through diet, exercise and inner work.

Your Psychic Says .....

You have an opportunity for truce-making, conflict resolution, negotiation and resolving important issues with people or things in your life. Don't lose anymore sleep over it. Dismiss your worries with a heartfelt prayer.

Your Psychic Says .....

Get it in writing! Take time to read the fine print. You are vulnerable, but by being cautious I see you escaping a difficult situation just in the nick of time.

Your Psychic Says .....

I see that you are worrying too much. Remember that worry is an interesting state of consciousness because it takes you to the future and it takes you to the past, and has you totally avoiding the present. You need to stay in the present and handle things as they come up, and not think about the "what ifs" of tomorrow, or the "if onlys" of yesterday.

Your Psychic Says .....

Today is the day to face the hard tasks. You have been putting things off for too long. Face the music. You need to put consistent energy into your personal and professional issues.

Your Psychic Says .....

This is the best time to generate new projects. Become aligned with people and situations that energize you rather than deplete you.

Your Psychic Says .....

Don't fear change, instead embrace it and take action for future happiness. A new phase of your life is now beginning whether you want it or not. But you are ready for turning over a new leaf. What I see will change your life for the better.

Your Psychic Says .....

I sense that you want to move too fast with a special someone, out of your own neediness. Slow down, this someone does not want you to get too close until they are ready. Don't ask too many questions...or tell too much for now.

Your Psychic Says .....

It's important to take care of yourself now and to pay attention to your feelings. You are forced to see that something is not working out. You have ceased to grow and the only answer is to walk away. I see you starting a fresh new chapter. You will find something more meaningful.

Your Psychic Says .....

I sense that you want to experience something new. You're getting the urge to cut those ankle chains right now. You have the choice of embarking on an exciting spiritual search, or at least developing a new interest.

Your Psychic Says .....

Don't fall into the trap of keeping yourself harmlessly busy by polishing the brass lamp, while avoiding what really needs to get done right now. Get focused on the task even if it demands a lot of you, like an accounting, reporting on your activities or making adjustments to please the powers that be.

Your Psychic Says .....

You are going to hear good news. Your stress is about to get lighter. Money suddenly comes to you from out of the blue… and it's just enough. Some of your accounts are cleared. The check arrives just in time.

Your Psychic Says .....

Watch your health. You're running yourself down lately trying to resolve problems. You need to put some effort into keeping yourself emotionally up. When you do, you will see things in a more positive light, from which solution will come. You'll also have more energy.

Your Psychic Says .....

Finally you will have some extra cash. When it comes, pull out your wallet for a little shopping spree. Spruce up your house, or have a big feed for the entire family and friends. Enjoy!

Your Psychic Says .....

Recognize that you are at the crossroads. Be clear on the ramifications of the situation. Carefully make good choices in order to further your own development, as well as to accommodate the needs of others in the situation. Listen to your gut.

Your Psychic Says .....

The best thing to do right now is nothing. Watch and wait for new developments, for you have done all that you can. Behind the scenes, I see good progress being made, but it is slow coming. Envision things getting just the way you want them.

Your Psychic Says .....

Your reality check is not coming in the mail, but from someone close to you. You are vulnerable at this moment so be careful of how much information you share with that person.

Your Psychic Says .....

History has a way of repeating itself. You need to study and learn from the past in general. Take the day to carefully analyze your situation and initiate a plan of action. You will discover a solution.

Your Psychic Says .....

I see a challenging situation where you use wisdom to express yourself intelligently. Communication is very important here. This is not a serious or long-term challenge.

Your Psychic Says .....

I sense that if you do not ease up on the gas pedal of life, you're about to find yourself spinning in circles. The roads you have chosen have led you to this point, and you now need to slow down. In doing so, you will achieve your personal best.

Your Psychic Says .....

Life is opening up. Your sense of hope is moving you toward your dreams. I see release from past difficulties. Whatever you initiate now will take a positive direction.

Your Psychic Says .....

You have either been ill or recently endured a stressful situation. But a period of relaxation will give you a chance to regroup with time to take care of your emotional and physical needs.

Your Psychic Says .....

You can now resolve something that has been nagging you for a long time. I see someone who cares about you helping a lot.

Your Psychic Says .....

Finally you will identify and correct the blocks standing between you and the great abundant life that you deserve. I see you exploring new ways of increasing your income to build the inflow higher than the outflow.

Your Psychic Says .....

Listen to your gut feelings or intuition, as that will be more accurate than your logic right now. But pay attention. Your intuition will lead you into positive life experiences.

Your Psychic Says .....

Your emotions are being vigorously stirred. You are not sure how things are going to work out. You feel like you are going nowhere, or things are about to close in on you. Don't give up. I see two great opportunities coming your way. Take one of them or both, if you feel you can handle them, and get back on track.

Your Psychic Says .....

Guard against arrogance or dealing with arrogant people. You must avoid one particularly vain and proud man. He will cause you trouble.

Your Psychic Says .....

Move cautiously in the sale or purchase of a home, or in renovating one. I see you wanting things to happen too fast, with impatience leading you into some big problems.

Your Psychic Says .....

A phase is definitely coming to an end. You will soon be able to look back over what has happened and evaluate those events. You can look forward to a reward or a promotion from your past efforts.

Your Psychic Says .....

It looks to me like you've been asleep at the wheel of your life. Instead of feeling stuck, it is time to wake up and recognize that you have choices. It will take thinking and some action to shape your future.

Your Psychic Says .....

You are working too hard at getting what you want. Know that visualizing is your most effective tool for getting end results. The clearer you are visualizing what you're wanting, the sooner you will bring your visualization into reality. Let the Universe take care of the "how".

Your Psychic Says .....

Give recognition and acknowledgment to the people who add richness to your life, and insist on having friends who also recognize and acknowledge you. Make it a habit of cultivating strong relationships. Never underestimate the power of positive people around you.

Your Psychic Says .....

Somebody is pressuring you to make a decision quickly. There is no rush. Slow down. Don't act impulsively just to please someone. If it's not your own honest decision it will later bring you regrets.

Your Psychic Says .....

Butting heads with individuals, who are more stubborn than you, can leave you with a migraine. You are far more likely to achieve a successful outcome if you use diplomacy in your dealings with others. If you think peaceful thoughts, you'll feel peaceful emotions. Then you can expect people to be more receptive to you. The immediate results will be a sense of peace instead of a headache.

Your Psychic Says .....

You feel a great sense of optimism about the future. You're right, you will soon experience a change of fortunes for the better. Have faith in the future. Everything will turn out for the best.

Your Psychic Says .....

Look at how far you have come and what you have achieved so far. You are ready to immerse yourself in the good things of life. I see you securing a more comfortable way. Get in touch with your own nature and enjoy the moment.

Your Psychic Says .....

I can see that it has been too long since you took a walk in the mountains. Think not? Well, how about watching squirrels scamper up a tree, or just plain following a stream by the meadow flowers? Or how about walking the beach, noticing sand pipers and sea gulls, while the waves fill the air with sound. When did you do this last? In other words, how long since you just let it all go, and took in the beauty of this earth, including the baby blue sky? Don't wait any longer. Your soul is hungry.

Your Psychic Says .....

You need to be careful about making rash or impulsive decisions today. You are fired up and eager to get going - you don't want to waste any time. But you better take time and listen to your intuition.

Your Psychic Says .....

A letter is coming that you are not expecting. It is coming from afar. The contents will be quite a surprise. Good news.

Your Psychic Says .....

I sense that your body is in need of good nutritious food. Eating on the run is taking a toll that you can't see now, but it is going to show up soon. Don't ignore the health signs.

Your Psychic Says .....

You're coming out from a contemplative period, feeling insecure. But in spite of that, you're willing to take risks. Good for you! New ambitions are forming that will lead to new goals.

Your Psychic Says .....

Change is inevitable, so you might as well go with the flow. You now have all of the tools needed to make this change. Move ahead, take charge of the situation. It is offering you hope to create a great future. Don't let negative and fearful thoughts block you from this new beginning.

Your Psychic Says .....

Lately you have been anxious, and a full night's sleep is hard to come by. I sense that the thoughts keeping you awake are not really the root of the problem. Within a few days you will discover what is really bothering you.

Your Psychic Says .....

You are entering a cycle in life when people just seem to give you things. Best of all, you are surrounded by those who love you. In any case, appreciate this wonderful cycle of your life.

Your Psychic Says .....

It's a great day to make a wish. Everything is working out just the way you planned, with the Universe giving you a "jump start". Your life is moving into an upward cycle.

Your Psychic Says .....

Look around you. Who needs some kind words? Give this person a lift. Send a card or a note. It will make their day and yours too.

Your Psychic Says .....

As usual you're not taking time to relax and balance out your fast moving, high stress life. You do too much, too fast and too often. I see you finally learning to say "no", and bringing your life into better balance. But it's up to you.

Your Psychic Says .....

You have been neglecting your spiritual side. Listen to your inner voice. Acknowledge the existence of a higher power and allow yourself to rely on it for support. It's hard to create conditions as you like them without the support of the Universe. Meditate more, and pay attention to the thoughts that give you a lift.

Your Psychic Says .....

Notice where you walk. There may be a coin lying on the ground. Don't pass it up. You'll be glad you did. A message from above comes with it.

Your Psychic Says .....

I see you finding new wisdom as you review the past year. You'll extract some great concepts that will serve you well. Share these ideas with someone you trust.

Your Psychic Says .....

Back to worrying too much, huh? It will send your mind down a rabbit hole again. I sense that you need to spend a lot more time celebrating what you have. If you will keep your mind on that, you'll find that many people will want to celebrate life with you.

Your Psychic Says .....

Being an astute observer gives you the advantage you've needed to excel in an important area of your life. Along with doing very well, you are appreciated in ways that are starting to show.

Your Psychic Says .....

You'll feel like indulging yourself today. Your hunger for food, love and celebrating can feel completely innocent and natural, and it is. It's ok. Go ahead and have fun.

Your Psychic Says .....

If you're single, the chances are high that you will connect with someone you have already met, but whom you suddenly see in a totally new light. If you're married, expect your sweetie to be more romantic.

Your Psychic Says .....

There is enormous potential for renewal in your life as passion motivates you to throw out old stuff restraining you from moving ahead. Take time to get serious and map out a strategy. Have an "I can do anything" attitude, and it will take you much closer to what you desire.

Your Psychic Says .....

You need to pay more attention to your health and diet in order to feel better. Take time to have a well deserved rest. Be your own spiritual gardener, and plant the seeds for good health by changing some old habits. I sense that soon, you'll have great energy and you'll bring some fun into your life.

Your Psychic Says .....

You have been feeling trapped, stuck in a rut and unable to change things. The energy is now changing. You are in the mood to be adventurous and have some fun. As you come in tune with yourself, you'll be able to move mountains. So it is a good time to do things that you would have never dared try before. You are not held back anymore.

Your Psychic Says .....

It's a great time to start a work project or go for some other area of interest that inspires you. This is the day to act on your intuition and move forward.

Your Psychic Says .....

The circumstances may look challenging at the moment, but you should not be discouraged by your present setbacks. Someone in a position of power may help you financially, or you may do it through your own efforts. Either way, I see rewards.

Your Psychic Says .....

Trying to force things will only backfire, leaving you feeling small. It's not easy to swallow your pride but you need to accept the reality of things. Your feelings are strong but you will avoid a delicate situation by learning to say things in a more gentle way.

Your Psychic Says .....

Your mind and your time are precious, so weed out those worries you can't do anything about now. Focus your attention on where you can create positive change in the next few weeks. Be careful about taking on more than you can do, or taking on the work of others.

Your Psychic Says .....

The situation calls for an immediate response. There is really no time to think it over and it's probably better that way. You must spring into action with enthusiasm. It is now or never, you see.

Your Psychic Says .....

Stay on top of things. Batten down the hatches and go full steam. The air is charged with politics but it's all subject to which way the wind blows. So look out for changing weather conditions. As things take shape around you, get a foothold if you can. And at all times remember you are in charge of your own life.

Your Psychic Says .....

In the weeks ahead you can expect to discover someone of interest. Do not judge the book by its cover. Watch for someone with lasting values below the surface. Examine your own roots and make sure lasting values are there too.

Your Psychic Says .....

This is a day for bringing a spark of excitement to even the most routine situations. You are looking for some new ways to try your wings. For now, it is the experience itself that matters the most to you.

Your Psychic Says .....

You need to feel your own way, go with your instincts, follow your hunches and gut feelings. The answer you seek is within you. Meanwhile you will gain perspective by getting away from it all for a change of scenery.

Your Psychic Says .....

This is not the time to behave aggressively. Instead you should use diplomacy to achieve the desired results. Find a roundabout way of tackling things, rather than confronting them head-on. By doing so, you will secure an advantage. I see that clear, logical thinking will help you through.

Your Psychic Says .....

It is time to be yourself more, and dare to live your life the way you choose. This can feel scary, as you are not comfortable with abandoning what is familiar, even though you know you are on shaky ground. You will feel both liberated and alarmed by this experience, depending on how open to change you are.

Your Psychic Says .....

I see someone special in your life. Whether it is love or a business partnership, I sense that you will be able to rely on this person with great trust. This will be a relationship of equals.

Your Psychic Says .....

I see that somebody is trying to get in the way of your progress. You've worked too hard for this. Don't let anyone stop you now. Look at both the facts and the feelings, for this will enable you to be objective.

Your Psychic Says .....

You are feeling at a loss on how to proceed. For the time being, at least, your better choice is to stay where you are. As other stages develop, when and how to move forward will become clearer.

Your Psychic Says .....

You are often tempted to blame fate rather than taking responsibility for your life. You are embarking on a new chapter and it is up to you to determine whether this will be a positive or negative experience. Whatever you decide is the way it will be.

Your Psychic Says .....

You are entering a fruitful period that is rich with possibilities. It promises the satisfaction of achieving something worthwhile that will stand the test of time.

Your Psychic Says .....

You are now able to recognize the value of what you have, feeling a deep sense of material, spiritual, and emotional abundance. Being in a position to help others, you are happy to share your luck.

Your Psychic Says .....

You have a tremendous zest for life. You are overflowing with exciting ideas, ready for wherever your quest takes you. You have the ability to encourage others to strive beyond their own personal limits. Learn to trust your intuition even more.

Your Psychic Says .....

Be honest with what is going on. Avoid putting the blame on other people. You will be able to move on but only if you don't get stuck in resentment and denial.

Your Psychic Says .....

I sense that you, or someone close to you, is involved in a legal battle, but the time is soon right for an agreement to be negotiated. Stewing in silent resentment will hurt you. You will be given good advice.

Your Psychic Says .....

To remain healthy and happy, you need rest. For your life of ever increasing, crashing downpours of activity, this is the perfect time to escape. Take some time off, go on a vacation, or simply relax with a hobby. This is an excellent opportunity to nourish your soul.

Your Psychic Says .....

If you have been down on your luck, this bad phase will soon end and good fortune will soon begin. If things have been going well, they are about to get even better. What you have learned spiritually, you'll end up applying to all areas of your life.

Your Psychic Says .....

Pay attention to what is really going on around you, look closely at the motivation of others, and avoid the easy solution. You have what it takes. There is a short window of opportunity for you to make a decision.

Your Psychic Says .....

There is something new and exciting coming into your life. It can be in many forms. This will come about because something in you will react to a situation from your intuition, as opposed to your head.

Your Psychic Says .....

You will soon find great value in looking after number one, like proving that you have the right to gain what is due you. It is the right time to ask for something you believe you deserve. You will get it sooner than you think.

Your Psychic Says .....

You are feeling positive, so make the most of it. Love the one you're with, and iron out the difficulties. There is a sense of harmony inside you that will rub off on those close to you.

Your Psychic Says .....

Whether through prayer, meditation or other practices, show your gratitude for the gifts you have been given, and for the people in your life. Feel good today.

Your Psychic Says .....

You are feeling frustrated. It does not help to let anxiety take over when you run into circumstances that are beyond your control. Relax and study the situation. A solution will present itself.

Your Psychic Says .....

You are working too hard. It is not so much that you need to slow down (that would drive you crazy). It is more that you should find a way to feed your soul as well as your pocket. This will go a long way toward melting away your stress.

Your Psychic Says .....

Lately, you've been running on fumes spiritually. Take time to meditate and fill up your spiritual can. Start with gratitude. By doing so, your entire attitude towards life, business, friendship and romance will change to a lighter, more positive outlook. You will then draw people and opportunities to you.

Your Psychic Says .....

If you are unmarried and seriously seeing someone, the subject of matrimony will start to enter your conversations. It is a good time to consider making your partnership a permanent one. If you are currently married I see a strengthening of your bonds.

Your Psychic Says .....

This is not the best time for you to make major changes in your life. Doing so may complicate things or potentially damage them. It is best to wait and let events unfold. Your intuition will lead you to understand the problem. From that will come the solution.

Your Psychic Says .....

You have a lot to look forward to and are in an enviable position. I see you getting some extra money. It could be a windfall or simply a nice gift. It is also an excellent time to pay off your old debts.

Your Psychic Says .....

Keep on having an optimistic attitude. Some news is about to come to you in the nicest way. You will regain your confidence and your motivation. I see that you will experience peace of mind, enjoy a better sense of who you are, and where you are going.

Your Psychic Says .....

I see a pleasure trip coming up that is not for business or out of necessity. You will not be going alone this time. It is a family vacation, or a holiday from work with a friend. Enjoy the time off.

Your Psychic Says .....

Your sense of self-worth is on the rise. Where it leads will depend on your vision of where you are going. Finish your current plan first and then start thinking about the next one.

Your Psychic Says .....

You are inspired to make a move. Trust your intuition to guide you toward the right place. If you carry the burden of fear, now is the time to let it go. Fear of moving or taking action can influence your decisions to your detriment.

Your Psychic Says .....

A business partnership or a romantic relationship needs to be treated with the respect it deserves. The mutual support you will give each other will be very important to both of you in order to succeed.

Your Psychic Says .....

It is fine to be generous with your time and resources, but don't spread yourself too thin today. Take a moment or two to experience the happiness of being with people you care about.

Your Psychic Says .....

Because of some obstacles now, it is an excellent time for you to show your own flexibility. You will need to compromise or bend a little but the outcome will be all that you want it to be.

Your Psychic Says .....

Expect a miracle in your life. I see one coming!

About the Author

JOHANNE VERVILLE-HUFFAKER was born in Quebec, Canada where very early in life she experienced her gift as a psychic. At the time she thought everyone could see the future, read other people's thoughts, feel their emotions, and even connect with the "other side". She soon learned that her gifts were indeed unique. With it came an understanding that these uncommon abilities were not to make her own life easy— it was for providing others with foresight and knowledge they did not have, often crucial for putting their life on course.

Having sessions with her clients has been her passion and fulfillment for the past two decades, where her on-target psychic readings have been of inestimable value. This has even included working with police departments where her vision of the crime scene provided the missing link to information leading to arrest and conviction.

Her practice is centered in Palm Springs, where California clients come for private consultation, as well as those flying in from out of State. But the breadth of her clientele is throughout America and many foreign lands, where they connect with her by telephone. Johanne also speaks fluent French, which extends her presence into French speaking countries.

When she is not seeing clients, you can find her with her husband, Dale Huffaker, at their beach house in

Huntington Beach, writing, or busy with the next travel event.

Johanne has several writings in various stages of completion. As finished, each will be featured on her website.

You may contact Johanne through her website at :

www.joverville.com.

CPSIA information can be obtained at www.ICGtesting.com
Printed in the USA
BVOW08s1548251113

337286BV00001B/1/A

9 781434 330475